These are the beliefs
Which every Muslim must believe

عَلَيْهِمُ السَّلَام
الأنبِياء
THE PROPHETS

About Sayyidna Al-Mustafa
And all the other prophets of Allah

SING ALONG

"صلواتُ ربِّ العالمينَ
على الأنبِياء والمُرسَلينَ"

"Salawatu Rabbil-
Aalameena
Alal-anbiya'i
Wal-mursaleena"

Every prophet, he must possess
Four qualities with which they're all blessed

- الصَّدقُ
  - Truthfulness
- والأمانة
  - Trustworthiness
- التَبليغ
  - Conveying the Message
- والفَطانة
  - Cleverness

Truthfulness, and trustworthiness
Conveying the message, and cleverness

SING ALONG

"صلواتُ ربِّ العالمينَ
على الأنبياء والمُرسَلينَ"

"Salawatu Rabbil-Aalameena
Alal-anbiya'i
Wal-mursaleena"

The prophets are always truthful
And with Allah's light, their hearts are always full

١
الصِّدقُ
TRUTHFULNESS

They tell the truth in matters big and small
They tell the truth when they're young and when they're old

SING ALONG

"صلواتُ ربِّ العالمينَ على الأنبِياء والمُرسَلينَ"

"Salawatu rabbil-aalameena alal-anbiya'i wal-mursaleena"

The prophets must be trustworthy
Since of Allah's trust, they must be worthy

② الأمانة
TRUSTWORTHINESS

They can never ever commit a sin
They are pure from without, and pure from within

SING ALONG

"صلواتُ ربِّ العالمينَ على الأنبِياء والمُرسَلينَ"

"Salawatu rabbil-aalameena alal-anbiya'i wal-mursaleena"

The prophets must be able
To convey the message to the people

٣
التَبليغ
CONVEYING THE MESSAGE

They must deliver what Allah has revealed
Without a word forgotten, or a word concealed

SING ALONG

"صلواتُ ربِّ العالمينَ
على الأنبِياء والمُرسَلينَ"

"Salawatu rabbil-
aalameena
alal-anbiya'i
wal-mursaleena"

The prophets must be clever

Since it's Allah's guidance, that they must deliver

4

الفَطانَة

CLEVERNESS

They must be bright, they must be smart

For them to change minds, for them to ease hearts

SING ALONG

"صلواتُ ربِّ العالمينَ على الأنبِياء والمُرسَلينَ"

"Salawatu rabbil-aalameena alal-anbiya'i wal-mursaleena"

salawat Nasheed

salawat Nasheed

It's possible for prophets to go through
What others go through, people like me and you

الجائِزَ في حَقِّهِم
WHAT IS POSSIBLE FOR THEM TO EXPERIENCE

Like hunger and sleep, loss and gain
Marriage and divorce, pleasure and pain

SING ALONG

"صلواتُ ربِّ العالمينَ
على الأنبِياءِ والمُرسَلينَ"

"Salawatu rabbil-aalameena alal-anbiya'i wal-mursaleena"

It's also possible for them to fall ill
With a light kind of illness, if you will

الجائِزِ في حقِّهِم
WHAT IS POSSIBLE FOR THEM TO EXPERIENCE

But their illness is never of the serious kind
That can drive people away, or affect the prophet's mind

SING ALONG

"صلواتُ ربِّ العالمينَ
على الانبِياء والمُرسَلينَ"

"Salawatu rabbil-
aalameena
alal-anbiya'i
wal-mursaleena"
♪♬

According to most scholars

The prophets exceed angels in honor

فاضَلوا المَلائكة
THEY EXCEEDED THE ANGELS IN RANK.

And Prophet Muhammad is their Imam

And the angels upon him send salams

SING ALONG

صلواتُ ربِّ العالمينَ
على الأنبِياء والمُرسَلينَ

"Salawatu rabbil-aalameena alal-anbiya'i wal-mursaleena"

All Muslims must pay attention
And believe in all the prophets with no exception

الإيمان
بالأنبِياءِ كَافَّة
BELIEVE IN ALL THE PROPHETS

Especially those mentioned in the Qur'an
You should know their names, and by heart if you can

SING ALONG

"صلواتُ رَبِّ العالمينَ
على الأنبِياء والمُرسَلينَ"

"Salawatu Rabbil-Aalameena
Alal-anbiya'i
Wal-mursaleena"

ADAM

Sayyidna Adam (ﷺ) is the father of all human beings and the first prophet on earth. Allah (ﷻ) created him in heaven from earthly mud. Allah (ﷻ) taught him the names of all things. Except for satan, all the angels prostrated to him. As a punishment, Allah (ﷻ) sent Sayyidna Adam (ﷺ) and his wife Sayyidah Hawa down to earth, after they ate from the forbidden tree in heaven!

IDREES

Sayyidna Idrees (ﷺ) was the first tailor by trade. It is said that Allah (ﷻ) taught him astrology, mathematics, and other types of knowledge, making that his miracle. He was also the first to use the pen. He was the first descendant of Sayyidna Adam (ﷺ) and of Sayyidna Sheith (ﷺ), who was honored with Prophethood.

Sayyidna Nuh (ﷺ) is a prophet and a messenger. He is the grandson of Sayyidna Idrees (ﷺ). He was a carpenter by trade. His people worshipped idols, and they rejected his message. He lived for 950 years calling his people to Allah (ﷻ). His people made fun of him and abused him. Before the great flood, he was ordered to build the ark, which saved him and those who believed in him from drowning.

Prophet Hud (ﷺ) was the first Arab prophet. He was sent to the tribe of 'Aad in Yemen. The people of 'Aad were very strong giant people. They built a great city called Iram in southern Oman. They worshipped idols and rejected Sayyidna Hud (ﷺ). Allah (ﷻ) sent upon them a great wind that destroyed them. Prophet Hud's (ﷺ) tomb is in Yemen.

Prophet Salih (ﷺ) is an Arab prophet. He is a descendant of the great prophet Nuh (ﷺ). He was prophet to the nation of Thamud who lived in Al-Hijr, in Arabia. His miracle was the giant she-camel that appeared from within a large rock. His people rejected his message. They were punished with thunderbolt, after they killed the she-camel.

Sayyidna Lut (ﷺ) was the nephew of Sayyidna Ibrahim (ﷺ), and the first one to believe in him. Allah (ﷻ) sent him to the people of Sodum, located near the Dead Sea. They were evil people who were committing very bad sins. Prophet Lut's wife was siding with those people against her husband. Allah (ﷻ) sent His angels and destroyed them, along with the wife of Sayyidna Lut (ﷺ).

Sayyidna Ibrahim (ﷺ) is the father of the prophets. He was mentioned in the Quran 69 times. He was an orphan raised by his uncle Aazar. He was also given the Suhof (Scrolls) to help him guide his nation to Islam. His people were idol worshippers who rejected him. He was thrown in the fire for destroying the idols of his people. Allah (ﷻ) saved him from the fire of Nimrod. He built the Ka'aba with Sayyidna Isma'il (ﷺ), and called people to Hajj.

Sayyidna Isma'il (ﷺ) is the first son of Sayyidna Ibrahim (ﷺ). He was a true worshipper of Allah (ﷻ), and the loving son of Sayyidna Ibrahim (ﷺ). He was raised in Mecca by his mother Hajar, after Sayyidna Ibrahim was ordered to leave them in the desert. Allah ordered his father to sacrifice him, but then sent down a ram to be sacrificed instead. That is one of the reasons we celebrate Eid Al-Adha every year.

The second son of Sayyidna Ibrahim (ﷺ), and the father of prophet Ya'qub (ﷺ). His mother was Sarah, the first wife of Sayyidna Ibrahim (ﷺ). She had him when she was 90 years of age. This miracle was mentioned in the Quran. Allah sent the angels to inform Sayyidna Ibrahim (ﷺ) and his wife that Allah was gifting them Sayyidna Ishaq (ﷺ). He travelled in Sham calling people to Allah (ﷻ).

Sayyidna Ya'Qub (ﷺ) is the son of Sayyidna Ishaq (ﷺ). He was also known by the name of Isra'il. He had 12 sons including Sayyidna Yusuf (ﷺ). He was born in Palestine. During his lifetime, he travelled to the north of Iraq, returned to Palestine and eventually settled in Egypt where he passed away. According to his final wishes, he was buried in Palestine.

Sayyidna Yusuf (ﷺ) is the son of sayyidna Ya'Qub (ﷺ). The Quran tells his story in a surah named Yusuf. His brothers tried to get rid of him because he was his father's favorite son, and they were jealous. He was a true man of Allah (ﷺ) who went through lots of hardship, but remained loyal and true to the religion of his fathers. He was the reason why the children of Isra'il moved to Egypt.

Sayyidna Shu'aib (ﷺ), is another Arab prophet. Many scholars believe that Sayyidna Shu'aib (ﷺ) was the elderly man who offered safety to Sayyidna Musa (ﷺ), when he fled Egypt. He lived in Madyan in Saudi Arabia. His people earned their living by cheating people. They rejected Sayyidna Shu'aib's (ﷺ) message. They were punished by a cloud carrying fire.

AYYUB

Prophet Ayyub (ﷺ) was a nephew of Prophet Ya'qub (ﷺ). He is known for his patience. Allah (ﷻ) tested him with many difficult tests. He took everything from him, including his health, but he never complained. His illness was difficult, but it was not of the type that make people run away from him. After passing his tests, Allah (ﷻ) gave him back more than what he took from him.

DHUL KIFL

Sayyidna Dhul Kifl (ﷺ) is a prophet of Allah (ﷻ). His name is mentioned twice in the Qur'an. Historians believe that Dhul Kifl (ﷺ) is the Israelite prophet Ezekiel who is also known as Ḥazqiyal in Arabic. The Quran mentions him as being one who is patient, righteous, and one of Allah's (ﷻ) chosen servants.

Sayyidna Musa (ﷺ) is a prophet and a messenger. He is the descendent of Sayyidna Ya'qub (ﷺ). His book is the Torah. He was raised by Aasiyah, the wife of pharaoh. He defeated the magicians of pharaoh with the two miracles Allah (ﷻ) gave him. He also split the sea with his staff, and led the Israelites out of slavery in Egypt. He received the Ten Commandments on Mount Sinai.

Sayyidna Harun (ﷺ) was the older brother of sayyidna Musa (ﷺ). He was born 5 years before Sayyidna Musa (ﷺ). Sayyidna Musa (ﷺ) asked Allah (ﷻ) for his brother to become his helper. Allah (ﷻ) granted Sayyidna Harun (ﷺ) prophethood, and made him the helper of Sayyidna Musa (ﷺ). Allah (ﷻ) then gave them the mission to deliver the children of Isra'il out of slavery in Egypt.

داوود
DAWUD

Sayyidna Dawud (ﷺ) is a descendent of Judah, one of the twelve sons of Sayyedina Ya'qub (ﷺ). As a kid he defeated Jalut the giant in battle. Az-Zabur was the book revealed on to him. He was given such a beautiful voice, that even the mountains and the birds sang Allah's praises with him. He was the first to make battle armor from iron. He used to fast every other day.

سُليمان
SULAIMAN

Sayyidna Sulaiman (ﷺ) is the son of Sayyidna Dawud (ﷺ). He was granted a kingdom like no other. Many served him, including Jinn, the wind, and birds. He could speak and understand the language of birds and animals. He commanded the Jinn to restore masjid Al-Aqsa in Palestine. His vast armies were made of men, Jinn, birds and animals.

ILYAS

Prophet Ilyas (ﷺ), or Elijah in Hebrew, was sent to guide the children of Isra'il. He was given the prophetic mission to stop them from worshipping idols. Some Islamic scholars believe, that Ilyas (ﷺ) is from the descendants of Sayyidna Harun (ﷺ). The majority of Ilyas's (ﷺ) people rejected his teachings. Prophet Alyasa' (ﷺ), his student, continued the mission of Ilyas (ﷺ).

ALYASA'

Sayyidna Alysa' (ﷺ) is a prophetAllah (ﷺ). He was also the pupil of Sayyidna Ilyas (ﷺ). After Sayyidna Ilyas (ﷺ), he continued the mission of preaching to the people. He is buried in Diyar Bakr in Turkey. Because of flooding, his tomb was exhumed in 1994, and it was moved to higher ground. Witnesses say that his body was intact as if he was buried recently.

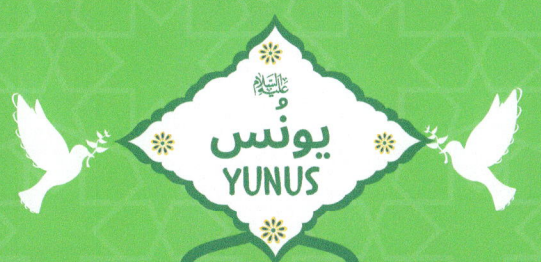

Prophet Yunus (※) is mentioned several times in the Qur'an as a prophet of Allah (※), and as Dhul-Nun (※). He was sent to the people of Nineveh in Syria. Without permission, he quit preaching to them and boarded a ship. He drowned and was swallowed by a whale. After repenting, Allah (※) released him from the whale. He went back to his people, and they all accepted Islam.

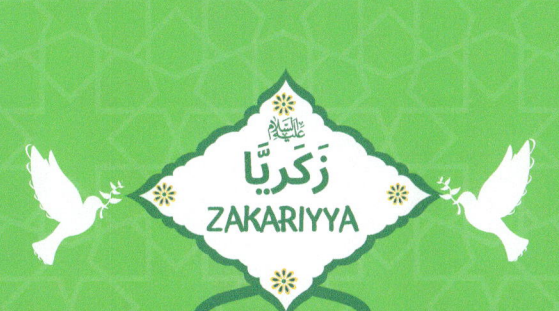

Prophet Zakariyya (※) is the descendent of sayyidna Sulayman (※). He served as the Imam of Masjid al-Aqsa in Jerusalem. He was the guardian of Sayyidah Maryam. Allah (※) granted him and his wife in their old age a son, sayyidna Yahya (※). Sayyidna Yahya (※) was also a prophet. Both of them were martyred by the children of Isra'il for speaking the truth.

Prophet Yahya (ﷺ) is the son of sayyidna Zakariyyah (ﷺ), and the answer to his prayer. Sayyidna Yahya (ﷺ) was ordered to hold fast to the scripture, and he was given wisdom by Allah (ﷻ) while still a child. He was dutiful towards his parents and he was not arrogant or rebellious. He was martyred for speaking the truth. His grave is in Damascus, in the Umayyad mosque.

Sayyidna 'Isa (ﷺ) is a prophet of Allah (ﷻ). He was miraculously born without a father. His mother is Sayyidah Maryam. He was sent to the children of Isra'il. His book is the Injil (Bible). He gave them the good news of the coming of sayyidna Muhammad ﷺ. His miracles included, speaking as a child, raising the dead, and healing the sick. His people tried to kill him. He was saved and raised to the 2nd heaven.

MUHAMMAD

Sayyidna Muhammad ﷺ is the last prophet and messenger to be sent to humanity. He is the seal of all the prophets, and the one carying their banner on judgement day. He was born in Mecca in the year of the elephant. Allah (ﷻ) sent him as "Mercy to the Worlds", and his message is for all of humanity. The book Allah (ﷻ) revealed on to him is the Qur'an. The Qur'an is his greatest living miracle. The Qur'an was delivered to him through Sayyidna Gibreel. He is the Imam of all the prophets and messengers. On the night of Isra' and Miraj, he lead them all in prayer in Jerusalem. On that night journey, he visited Jerusalem, the 7 heavens and beyond to Qaba Qawsain (two bows length or nearer). He was shown the heavens, the hells and the state of the people inhabiting them. He is the only prophet who was given the great shafa'ah (intercession) on judgement day. On that day, all nations will go to him asking him to intercede for them, and he will. Two thirds of the people entering heaven will be from his nation. His grave is in Medinah.

About this Book

Bismillah Ar-Rahman Ar-Raheem and peace and blessings upon Sayyidna Muhammad, his family, and his companions.

Aqida (Islamic beliefs) is the most important and essential knowledge amongst all religious knowledges. It is the foundation of one's religion. Understanding the correct Islamic beliefs regarding Allah, His prophets, and the unseen world, is the duty of every accountable Muslim. Aqidah linguistically is derived from the root aqada. In Arabic, one states, "aqada the rope" when the rope is tied firmly.

A modern example of the importance of having correct beliefs is the GPS system we use for navigation. Entering the correct address means we will arrive at the right destination, while entering the wrong address means we will arrive at a wrong destination.

Understanding the correct Islamic beliefs will help Muslims avoid making grave mistakes which can make their Islam null and void. Mistakes such as believing Allah resides in a place, or believing that prophets commit sins.

In this book, we will explain the four attributes which every prophet must possess in order to be a prophet of Allah. We will also explain the things that they share with the rest of us, and are permissible for them to experience as human beings.

We have also included short biographies of each of the 25 prophets and messengers mentioned in the holy Quran.

The information in this book is based on the explanation of "Aqidatul Awam" (Beliefs of the unlearned Muslims) composition by shaykh Ahmad Al-Marzouqi.

We understand that the subject of Islamic beliefs is a difficult subject for young minds to grasp. And although we tried as much as we could to simplify these books for kids, it may still take them some time to fully understand some of these concepts.

By writing this series, we tried to follow the example of Aqidah scholars who wrote rhyming (sing-along) compositions about Islamic Aqidah (beliefs). Kids through out the Muslim world would learn these compositions by heart, even before they fully understood them. The intention behind such compositions is to plant the seeds of correct Islamic beliefs in the minds and hearts of little Muslims.

This is the 2nd book
of a three books series explaining the
essential Islamic aqidah (beliefs) to kids.
The 1st book explains the Islamic beliefs
regarding Allah, while the 3rd book
will explain the Islamic beliefs
regarding the unseen, such as heavens
and angels.

We hope that these books will help
your kids to learn and understand the
correct Islamic beliefs, which will
become a foundation for them to lead a
meaningful religious life.

Other books by Itsy Bitsy Muslims

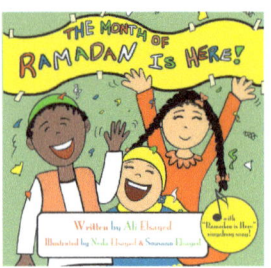
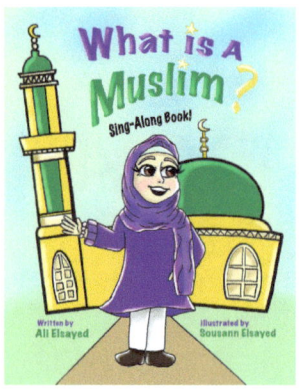
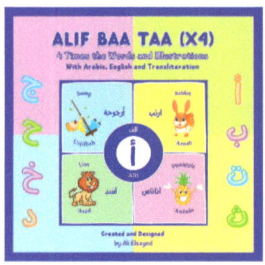

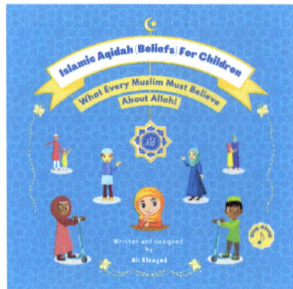
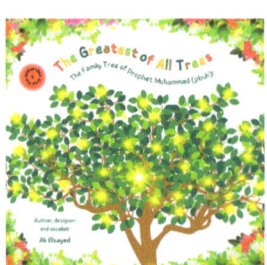

**For more children's books
and sing-alongs visit us**
@Itsybitsymuslims.com

Or scan QR code

If you like this book,
Please help us promote it by
leaving us a review on Amazon

www.ingramcontent.com/pod-product-compliance
Lightning Source LLC
Chambersburg PA
CBHW042147200426
43209CB00065B/1738